# Giving Yourself Permission:
## Reclaim Your Life After Sexual Assault

SHANEEQUA CANNON

# DEDICATION

This book is dedicated to my family. Without them, I would have never had the space, time, and opportunity to realize my dream of being an author "some day". This book is also dedicated to my late grandfather for instilling that dream in me. I had no idea when some day would come but it came at the perfect time-- God's time.

# CONTENTS

# ACKNOWLEDGMENTS

A sincere thank you to Dr. Tracy Timberlake and Nicole Walters, my mentors and coaches, who impressed upon me the importance of my message and the need for getting it out into the world.

# PREFACE

In America, rape culture is everywhere; it's in our music, movies, and magazines. Often girls are told that they are no more than bodies and they have no control or say so over their body. This message isn't always delivered verbally but it is heavily present in the images we push towards these youngsters. Wear your skirts a little shorter. Wear your hair rumpled as if you just got out of bed. Make sure you have kissable lips. Push up your breasts so that they're noticeable. Inject your rear so that it's prominent. Bleach your hair. Wear waist trainers for that hourglass figure.

And the control doesn't stop there. Being a female in America means that piles of guilt and shame are dumped upon your shoulders just because you were born a female. If a guy hits you, he loves you so why would you leave? If you sleep with him on the first date, you're a slut. If you make him wait, you're a tease. You can't expect him to be monogamous because "boys will be boys". You must abstain at all times. If you open your legs for someone you're not married to, you're a slut. If you go on birth control, you're a slut. If you get pregnant, you're not allowed to have an abortion. If you have a baby and you're unwed, you're a slut but do not ask for any assistance with taking care of that child because you should not

1

have been doing slut activities.

If you work full time to take care of your children and you miss school plays, you're a bad parent. If you take off time to go to school plays, you're a bad employee. If you're not there on time to hurry up and wait in the carpool line at school, you're a bad mom. If you need to leave a few minutes early, you'll have that talk about your position at your job.

If you try to do it all, you are shamed. If you try to stick to one thing, you are shamed. If you decide you don't want to have kids because you don't see how you can do it all, you are shamed. If you decide you want to have a big family, you are shamed.

We have a problem with the way we treat women in America. That problem begins from the very day girls are born. One of the places where this problem manifests the most is in the way we treat victims of sexual abuse. I understand that males are also victims of sexual abuse; that I cannot discredit but that I can't speak on. In this book I will be using a mixture of my own personal accounts plus facts and statistics from reputable sources. However, that does not mean this book cannot work for those of any gender identity reeling from the trauma of sexual abuse. This book is for everyone. Know that, when I refer to the way women feel, if you can identify, then I am talking to you as well.

We have a problem with the way we handle sexual abuse in America. Our laws are in favor of the perpetrator: the sentencing (hello Brock Turner!), the statute of limitations, the abortion laws-- none of them benefit the victims. But this book will not tackle policies and politics. That is for another conversation at another time. This book is about making sure you give yourself permission to live the best life you can possibly live despite and in spite of the circumstances.

# 1 AN INTRODUCTION

## Who Am I?

For the last 12 years, I've been a public high school teacher, working to inspire young individuals to envision a life of passion & purpose, to set attainable yet far-reaching goals, and to define life for themselves. My favorite moments were when I could connect the literature to real life. It wouldn't be unusual to find me using Ray Bradbury's *Sound of Thunder* to talk about the perils of suicide (every life matters, everything has a purpose) or Richard Connell's *The Most Dangerous Game* to talk about the need for humanity and how today's military-style video games make killing humans a sport rather than a taboo. Outside of those life meets literature moments, I wasn't happy with my career. Externally, I had a "good" job but internally I was struggling. I lived the life of a hypocrite, stamping down my own desires and dreams for the suffocating sense of duty that was placed on my shoulders over 20 years ago.

## What's my story?

In December 1995, I left high school during a lunch break to visit my aunt who lived across the street from the campus.

That day would have been no different than the countless days that came before it as eating lunch at my aunt's house was my routine. But that day in December, when my aunt wasn't home, marked the day I surrendered my power to someone who exerted his over me. He was bigger, taller, stronger. He was also my cousin, or so I thought. Turned out he was not a blood relative but he was someone I grew up calling cousin, someone who was close enough to me that being so physically close to me, in me, should not have crossed his mind. Before the lunch break was over, my life was forever altered. Not only had I been violated on my aunt's bed, my womb had also been plowed and conquered; his semen lay in wait for my egg.

Even though I physically got off the bed and went back to school, mentally I had been trapped on it by his steel grip on my self-worth, self-esteem, and self-confidence. My one attempt at telling a classmate ended with her laughing in disbelief because she knew my cousin and I subconsciously decided to never tell anyone again. Nearly nine months later, I went on to deliver the baby and raise him through the years when I struggled to take care of myself. I barely graduated from high school and flunked the first year and a half of college.

For a short while I became promiscuous, believing it gave me control over my body. After all, I said who; I said when; and I said where. I even went so far as to describe myself as a sex addict, a nymphomaniac when really all I was was a very broken individual incapable of giving myself the love and forgiveness I needed and deserved.

I floated through life, going wherever the wind took me. A teacher said, "Get therapy" so I did. The therapist said, "Apply for Academic Bankruptcy" so I did. That wiped my first two years of college clean and, when I got back into school, I landed into the safe structure of people telling me what to do. A few times, the carefree woman I truly was would peak through in small ways like going off to Spain for a study abroad program and leaving the School of Education to pursue my degree in English with a Creative Writing concentration.

But for the most part, I had no voice. I truly kept putting one foot in front of the other without much thought. Even when I wanted to abort my second child, I allowed others to talk me out of it, others who eventually had the procedure themselves. The moment on the bed affected me in all ways. I hid myself away from the pain, from the powerlessness, and from my purpose. My mind would fight and scream against what didn't sit right with my soul but I didn't speak up. I've had friends and family financially ruin me. I was scared to leave behind my "good" teaching job, which tried to finish destroying what little sense of value remained. I have been on all kinds of assistance-- cash assistance, food stamps, and Section-8. I've had two cars repossessed and I've been nearly evicted twice. I've made choices that never would have fit the person I am today, including the choices in partners, friendships, and relationships.

But I always kept moving forward with the slight hope that eventually my wanderings would develop direction. I've learned to say yes to opportunities which provide personal growth and experiences. While moving forward, I kept my eyes and ears open, listening and learning. Instead of continuing to resist my time as a teacher, I looked for the lessons-- what was I there to learn. In fact, it was during my planning period that I began writing and releasing myself from the stranglehold of being a rape victim, becoming, instead, a rape survivor.

In that empty classroom, I poured my tears and my memories onto paper, feeling all the emotions I locked up inside of myself that day on the bed. I felt the fear as it steamrolled through my body, causing my nerves to stand on end. I could hear the faint echoes of my mental screams bouncing off the walls of my skull. I felt the disbelief, the only emotion I allowed that day. It permitted the denial of what happened to persevere in spite of the growing evidence the rape had in fact taken place.

And I felt the anger, not only at my cousin for doing this to me or at my aunt for not being home or at the classmate who laughed. My biggest brunt of my anger was reserved for myself. If only I hadn't gone over there during lunch. If only I paid attention to the things he said like, "I like you." I naively thought he was joking. If only I listened to my mother and stayed away from that house all together.

Letting those feelings flood through me was cathartic because it allowed me to realize why I kept my mouth shut, why I didn't share what happened to me. I felt guilty for my role in what transpired as if it was my fault I was overpowered. I hid in my silence, wrapping myself in self-recrimination and shame and fear. I was always afraid that I would be blamed. I had to learn to let those feelings go because they were founded in a great untruth. Once I realized that it wasn't my fault, that I didn't rape me, the journey began the breaking of my silence.

First I read the story to my students. The after class chats of "Me too" or the silent sobbing of a student reliving the memories of her own sexual assault-- be it rape or molestation, disturbed me greatly. As I steered my students towards the counselor's office, it occurred to me there was a sense of the power and danger that lay behind sharing my story. It's a sisterhood to which I wished no woman belonged. And so I continued to share my story, hoping to be the person for my students that I never had for myself, the one who understood and helped them find help. But I never thought they would end up being the ones to school me.

I am a firm believer that Life is the greatest teacher; it hands us many lessons then tests us on them. And that was never truer for me than in my own classroom. Towards my last few years as a teacher, there was one question, couched as a statement, that kept coming up from the students: "Miss, you should be more than a teacher; you're not living up to your potential." I've always believed that our best and brightest should be the ones teaching the students; it's a shame how much the profession is devalued and undermined. But I knew the students weren't trying to upset me though they did. Those words affected me deeply and were a catalyst to awakening a fire within me. The sleepy dragon of self-worth stirred.

With every year that passed and every similarly uttered phrase, the dragon breathed life. Then came the ridiculous education policies and exams. The dragon tried out its unused legs. Then came the eviction notice and smoke curled from the dragon's nostrils. I fought off the eviction and I stayed indignant that I was in that predicament in the first place. But then came a second eviction notice the next year. Family members, as well as the low salary, contributed to my precarious financial situation. And so did I because I allowed that to happen. I refused to speak up, too scared to say, "No". That's what that moment on the bed taught me-- how to quiet my own voice, to devalue myself, and to allow others to take from me what should have been my choice to give.

That second eviction notice woke me up; the dragon breathed fire and I had enough-- enough of being undervalued, enough of being taken for granted, enough of being financially burdened, enough of working at something I didn't love and which was stressing me, instead of something I was crazy passionate about-- my writing. That summer I got fed up with the powerlessness. That summer I quit teaching. That summer I began living for me. But I was lost.

From the moment my choice was stolen from me over 20 years ago until the summer of 2015, I had no understanding of who I was or what I had to offer the world. When someone treats you as less than human, it robs you of not only your voice but your sense of self. Who was I to be treated as such on the bed, in my relationships, and in the teaching profession? Who was I to be used and shown time and time again that I was not worthy of compassion and protection and freedom? Who was I that I could only expect to give and give and give without any thought of demanding humanity and reciprocity?

Then Periscope happened. It was a new live streaming social media platform, just four months old at the time. I was enticed by and enthralled with the app's users' ability to talk to people all over the globe in real time, to learn from industry professionals for free, to watch women, especially women of color, leveraging the platform in such a way that they were regarded as experts in their field. And quite by accident the platform became an avenue for my story.

I intended to speak about the direct sales company I was a part of, to showcase the products and reach widely into my cold market. But one day the talk somehow turned to me being a survivor of rape and a member of my audience said, "Me too".

I was standing outside talking into my phone when I came to the realization that I had not given myself permission to get off of the bed. I was still there. I had not forgiven myself at all. With tears threatening to fall and my voice shakier than the grounds of California during an earthquake, I quickly ended that scope then sat in the car, stunned by that revelation.

And I was frightened, resistant to carve out my niche on this new social media platform on the basis of something that I would rather forget happened. I had moved on. I was over it. I loved my son; he was happy, healthy, and further in life than his father was at his age -- all without becoming a single parent on top of that. His dad and I were on speaking terms, especially since he stepped up as a father (this story to come later in my next book).

Though I had given up my apartment by not renewing my lease in order to thwart the eviction, life was good. I knew life could have been a heckuva lot worse than it was as I was told over and over again by people who knew my story. I didn't want to be cast as the girl who got raped. I didn't want to wrap myself back up in all the unearthed emotions that came with reliving the moment that was forever suspended in time. I wanted more for myself than that.

For weeks I ran away from what essentially was my purpose. But on the final day of my move, I discovered a CD containing a prophecy that was spoken over me back in 2005. Yes, the same year I began my journey writing the rape story in my first book, *However Long the Night*. On a random November night in 2005, the pastor of the church I attended singled me out to say that God was going to use me to speak to audiences of women and young girls in order to turn their hearts in a good way. That prophecy came with a caveat: I had to learn not to hate men. This pastor did not know me personally nor did he know my story. I bought the CD at the next service as a reminder of what God was going to do in my life. Fast forward 10 years and that's exactly what it was-- a reminder of the work that I was called to do.

**Why this book?**

So here I am, penning this book to help those of you who have gone through similar experiences as I have. Over the next few chapters, I hope to inspire you to not only get off the bed, but to give yourself the permission (and the forgiveness) to do so. Are you ready to put in the work? This won't be easy and results won't come overnight but I promise you it will be worth the work. And you deserve the peace it will bring.

# 2 TIME TO R.O.C.K.

Let me address the big elephant in the room. Sexual assault is something that is not uncommon. Sadly, it is an unfortunate club that many people belong to. According to the findings of the 2010 National Intimate Partner and Sexual Violence Survey, the statistics are that one in five women and one in seventy-one men will find themselves raped at some point in their lifetime. When talking sexual assault in general, which includes everything else as well as rape, the numbers are worse. One in four women and one in six men will be sexually assaulted before the age of 18. With nearly 320 million people in this country, that statistic converts into an unfathomable number of people who were and will be sexual assault victims.

So this is a truly unfortunate club that we belong to, however, these numbers are not to make you feel as if what happened to you was unimportant; these numbers are not to make you feel that what happened to you was okay. Because the truth is that it wasn't okay and you are important. No one's story is better or worse than yours. You experienced what you experienced and no one can invalidate that. It doesn't matter if you are ready to share your own story years later. It is your story. It happened to you. No one can tell you to stay silent.

So why this book? What is it that I want you to take from this book? I want you to rock.

Now the word "rock" has many connotations. We can take it in the literal sense in which a rock is a mass of sedimentary material that is compounded by particles until it is almost impenetrable. I don't want you to be that kind of rock. I don't want you to create a life in which you stuck and nothing can reach through to you to brighten up your life.

I want you to be the verb "rock", the do rock. I want you to live your life to the extremities of all that is positive and good like you deserve. I want you to rock in such a way that what happened to you only serves as a step up into your purpose. I want you to *rock*.

Now we're going to break down the word "rock" into its letters r-o-c-k. I have assigned a meaning to each letter. So let's start with the first letter, "r".

**Reclaim your life.**

Sexual assault does something to its victims that almost nothing else does. We are scarred in such a way that healing has to be a conscious act because the scars are so invisible that sometimes we don't even realize that our actions, our reactions are all because of that moment in time-- wherever that moment took place. For me that moment was on a bed in my aunt's house across from my high school during lunch. For you, it can be a myriad of other settings and times. The when and the where does not matter. What matters is that you give yourself permission to get up out of that situation and not just physically, because you've already done that part, but mentally, spiritually, and emotionally as well.

Are you still in that place mentally? Can you remember

the exact moment? Can you remember how it felt? Can you remember the music that was playing or the sounds that were being made? Can you remember? Are your senses still humming with the memory of what happened to you then? Are you mentally trapped in that moment?

I remember everything. I remember the bird outside the window. I remember the rankness of his breath. I remember the coils of the mattress pressing up against my back. And I remember the clamminess of his hands pressing against my wrists. I remember his weight. I remember retreating into my mind and hearing myself scream "No" even though I made not a single sound. For nearly twenty years, I had been mentally trapped.

As I write this with tears running down my face from that memory still, I know that I was also owned emotionally because one ounce of that memory would dredge up so many negative feelings about myself and about what happened. Without even knowing why, I failed the first year of college pretty much completely. Without even knowing why, I embraced my promiscuity, my self-proclaimed nymphomania as a legitimate part of who I was. Without even knowing why, my inability to focus, to think, and to feel were dismissed as unimportant yet frustrating personality traits. I locked all of that into my mind and I could not move forward.

Mentally, I was still on that bed, powerless, angry, scared, and disappointed. Yet, I was physically moving forward with life. I got a job. I graduated high school. I went on to college. Then I failed. My cousin still had power over me. My self-worth was locked under the vise grip he had on my wrists and my life. I didn't realize how important it was to make a conscious declaration that I would live life on my own terms, not as a person with vision clouded by the act of sexual assault but as a person with the strength to live and enjoy life despite the negative. I needed to reclaim my life.

## REFLECTION TIME

Examine your life to see if your vision is cloudy. Are you still emotionally trapped or are you standing in the power and realization that you are much more than that hurtful moment(s) in time? What did you want from your life before the assault? Who were you before the assault? What plans were you making before the assault? Do you still want to pursue them? If not, determine why not. If so, then examine what it would take to get back on track changed, better, stronger? As you work through this book and your life, it's a good idea to have a place, like a journal or a Word document, to explore your emotions and any noteworthy happening from your day.

_____

_____

_____

_____

_____

_____

_____

In order for me to reclaim my life and get back on track, I had to do this next thing, which was really *really* hard to do. But first...

**Own your story.**

As I told you before, I physically moved forward. Not only did I go back to college, I had a second kid; I went on to graduate from college; I became a teacher; I taught for ten years; I had two more kids, a set of twins; I completed my masters on the recovery bed after my C-section. So physically I kept moving forward. Physically I was fine. And if you asked me, emotionally I was fine too. And if you asked me, mentally I was too.

But I was not who I would have been had I not been raped. I gave over my power; I gave over my voice; I gave over my future; I gave over my dreams. But, on the outside to everyone else, I looked fine. It wasn't until I began my journey over ten years ago towards owning my story, that I began to *be* fine.

In 2005, I crafted the first pages of my autobiography, *However Long the Night.* I had to own what happened to me and not with a victim's mindset but as a person who logically looked at my life and went, "That is what happened, that is the result, this is where I am, and this is what I want and where I want to be". I had to own my story. I could not run from what happened, no matter how many degrees or how many children or how long I worked in a certain job. I was not fulfilled until I owned that story, until I said yes it happened but it will not define me.

While I was writing this book, a friend asked me, "If I didn't say yes but I didn't say no either even though I didn't want to have sex with him, was I sexually assaulted?" The simple answer to this question, without getting too complicated, is "Yes". If you didn't say yes, then it was no. Even if you participated in a make-out session, that did not imply permission to go all the way. Kissing might have felt good. Touching might have felt good. It's natural for the body to respond. But that didn't mean you wanted to give your whole body to the person in front of you.

The world has consent backwards. You don't have to say, "No". In fact, "No" is sometimes very hard to say because we fear rejection, retaliation, or, in some cases, for our lives. Or sometimes we question if we do want intercourse or how to say no to it and, during that time, our choice is stolen. But you do have to say, "Yes".

I'm going to repeat this: if you don't say yes, then it's no. And it doesn't matter what you were violated with—tongue, finger, toy, penis, etc. or who you were violated by—male, female, relative, friend, husband, date, stranger, boss, etc. This isn't about leading people on. It is *your* body, *your* choice. A kiss is only permission for a kiss. Touching is only permission for touching. If you don't give permission, then that person doesn't have the right to take you further than where you were willing to go. And, whether you were sober or drunk/high, if your choice was taken without your permission then you need to own your story: You were sexually assaulted.

Now owning your story is not about wallowing in pity or drowning in depression. Owning your story is about facing that truth. And owning that story is about not assigning blame to yourself. Yes, maybe you weren't supposed to be where you were; I was supposed to be at school. Yes, maybe your intuition said something was wrong; when I realized my aunt wasn't there, my spidey senses did start tingling but I didn't listen.

No matter what happened around you, someone else had a choice and he/she/they chose completely wrong. And the blame and shame for what happened lay at their feet. But you cannot stay angry; you cannot stay hurt; you cannot stay disappointed; and you cannot stay scared. A life lived with those emotions in control is not the life you deserve to live, unless you choose to stay mired in misery.

## REFLECTION TIME

What is your truth? How do you feel about it? If you need more space, feel free to write in your journal.

_____

_____

_____

_____

_____

_____

_____

_____

_____

_____

_____

_____

_____

_____

_____

_____

_____

_____

_____

_____

If you want to live a positive and fulfilling life, you have to own your story and reclaim your life. How does that happen?

Through this next part.

**Connect to something outside of yourself.**

What does it mean to connect to something outside of yourself? It means reaching out and asking for help, telling somebody. It means communicating with your friends, family, or other people who love you. It means seeking out a therapist who will listen to you in an objective manner and give you things that you could do toward helping yourself in your life. Now that doesn't necessarily mean medicine; medicine is useful where it is needed but sometimes you just have to do the hard work.

Connecting means getting out of your shell. Remember when we were talking about the literal meaning of rock, how all the minerals compounded until it solidified to the point where that mass becomes impenetrable? That's not what you need to be. That is a lonely place where your protection becomes your prison. It may be hard for things to penetrate your shell but it would also be hard for you to do the same.

You need to connect with humanity. You need to connect with therapists. You need to connect with your family. You need to connect with friends. You need to connect with the arts. Go see a show. Go see something that makes you feel, that takes you through the myriad of emotions so that you could spend the tears and then expel laughter. You need to go connect with nature. Sit on the beach and let the waves lap at your feet while you listen to the serenade of the seas. Or ride on a horse feeling its strength carry you faster than the wind that winds through its mane. Connect.

Get out of your house. Get out of your bed. Get out of your head and go connect. Find your talent. Find your passion. And then find your purpose. What feeds you? Connect. What heals you? Connect. What cleanses you? Connect.

I don't claim that making connections will be easy. Being vulnerable and open to experiences, as well as letting people in, can be scary and uncomfortable. But there's no growth in being comfortable. Chances are you've outgrown your old life. So instead of stuffing yourself into the old skin of your painful past, allow yourself to be momentarily open as you create a better life.

Your life is not a life to be lived alone and is not a life to be lived in the past. Not only do you need to keep moving forward, you need to connect along the way. So reclaim your life by owning your story and connecting to something outside of yourself.

## REFLECTION TIME

What are some ways you can create a connection? What are the things you enjoy doing or dreamed of doing? What are things you've put off for "someday"? How can you connect? What type of help do you need to move forward with your best life? Let the universe know so it can figure out how to provide.

_____

_____

_____

_____

_____

_____

_____

_____

---

_____

_____

_____

_____

_____

_____

_____

_____

_____

_____

_____

_____

So that brings us to the final point.

**Knock down all those negative thoughts.**

Whenever you feel doubt or anger or fear or anxiety or depression or any other negative emotion creeping into your space to block you from progress and purpose, you need to knock it down. Recognize the emotion for what it is, know where it's coming from, then knock it down.

One of the things I hadn't mentioned while sharing my story was the way people reacted to the news of my pregnancy. I understand that no parent wants their child to become a parent herself at just 17 years old but some of the things that were said to me stung. To this day, some of it still does. Those negative words didn't just come from my parents but from friends and other family members. I was told that I was stupid, that I was a failure, and that I would amount to nothing. I was told I was a disappointment. A cousin said that she no longer looked up to me. So on top of the rape and impending motherhood, I now had the weight of being a letdown on my shoulders. It's no wonder I cried every day during and in the months after my pregnancy. But I carried that negativity with me into so many different areas of my life. I wasn't worthy, deserving, or enough. That feeling still crops up every now and then and I have to consciously work to knock down that negativity with affirmations that I am worthy, deserving, and enough for this gift called life.

When I was able to identify why it was that I considered myself a nymphomaniac, I was able to put an end to the self-abuse. Due to the pervasiveness of the rape on my psyche, I attracted people who were not good for me, usually married or otherwise attached men. This left me feeling valueless and used, unworthy of a strong healthy relationship.

To combat those negative feelings, I implemented celibacy into my life while I mentally underwent reconstruction, which involved therapy and self-assessment. I removed myself from negative situations and friendships. I hung out with positive friends and found peace on the beach. Whenever depression loomed near, I went for walks, shedding pounds and negative self-talk. I felt sexy in an empowered way, healthy and strong. I was proud of my achievements and the change that was happening in my life. Now I've been in a healthy and supportive relationship for 6 years. Whenever I question if I deserve love, I remind myself of all the reasons I do. But this took time and practice.

## REFLECTION TIME

What are some of the negative habits you have? Where do they stem from? What would it take to break away from them? What messages play on the ticker tape of your mind? How can you rewrite those? What can you do to replace the negative with the positive?

_____

_____

_____

_____

_____

_____

_____

_____

_____

_____

_____

_____

_____

_____

_____

_____

_____

_____

_____

_____

_____

_____

_____

_____

_____

_____

Now I told you none of this was going to be easy and that it would not happen overnight but you need to rock.

**R**eclaim your life.

**O**wn your story.

**C**onnect to something outside of yourself.

**K**nock down the negativity.

I know how hurtful and debilitating it can be to have your body, mind, and soul violated by someone, especially someone you trust. But those people will go on with their lives with hardly a second thought about yours. Don't you think you deserve to go on with your life with _every_ thought about you? You were put on this earth to do something. You were put on this earth to _rock_.

# 3 THE CYCLE OF S.U.C.K.

This chapter is about what will happen if you do not rock. For some of you, what happened to you was many years ago. And for some of you, what happened to you was recent. Even though my incident was over twenty years ago, I got stuck in the Cycle of Suck. Now what is the Cycle of Suck?

The Cycle of Suck is a place where you do not allow yourself to be great, a place where you do not rock out your life. There is no reclaiming your life; there is no owning your story; there is no connecting to something outside of yourself; and there is definitely no knocking down the negative thoughts. In fact, the negative thoughts win more times than they lose.

Now some of us have gotten very good at camouflaging and pretending that we were not stuck in the Cycle of Suck. As I said earlier, if you looked at my life, you would have thought I was fine. After I was raped, I graduated from high school. Then I went on to college and I graduated from college with another child. Then I went on to teach for ten years and I graduated with my masters as a mother of four kids. I looked like I was doing well. But financially, I was almost bankrupt. In fact, I filed for bankruptcy in 2007.

Financially, I had to fight off eviction. Emotionally, I wasn't available to love. Now I love my kids, absolutely. And I don't say that as a given because I know that some people struggle with even that connection. And I will tell you, during the first couple of years as a mother, it was really hard to connect with my son and with others. But thank God for grace and that I was able to find it within myself to love my kids at least. But I can't tell you that I loved myself. And it wasn't because I had put on so much weight. It was because of the negative talk I consistently gave myself.

Just like we did with ROCK, let's break down SUCK.

**S**elf-sabotage

The **U**ns

**C**an't

**K**eeping Out

## Self-sabotage

I was self-sabotaging my relationships, my finances, and my dreams. My relationships weren't real. If they required work, I left. If they required me to give up part of myself, I left. If they required me to tear down that wall I put up after the rape, I left. I was so closed off and unavailable to love that I didn't feel lovable myself.

Remember when I mentioned earlier that I had help getting into my dire financial situations? The truth is, if I had loved myself at the time, I would have stood up for myself; I would have exercised the power of "No" instead of the "Yes" that was taken as being inherent with silence. I would have taken better care of myself, even financially. I allowed others' wants to trump my needs. And I talked to myself in such a way that I felt selfish for wanting to say no. I felt guilty for wanting to protect myself. You can't tell me that isn't a residual effect of that rape.

Self-sabotage also occurred in my dreams. I've always wanted to be a writer, always. My earliest memories are of the stories that I created. Some of those stories I won awards for in our county fair-- those $5 awards, let me tell you, were a big deal. But I did nothing with my writing, even after getting a creative writing degree. I would start stories once hot with an idea then stop. Start then stop. This was my pattern. So many stories unfinished. In fact, the autobiography I alluded to earlier, *However Long the Night*, was started back in 2005 and it took ten years before I got the drive to finish it. I would come up with every other reason, every other thing to do but to sit at my computer and write. The truth of the matter was I didn't need my computer to write; I could have used old school technology, pen and paper, and yet I never took the time to do it. I self-sabotaged.

I have another story I started in 2005-- totally different; it's a fictional romance. And I took over ten years to finish that one as well. I only wrote, not in moments of inspiration, but when I knew someone was looking. Also in 2005, I entered a masters program for Screenwriting; I wrote a screenplay I was truly proud of and I still haven't done the rewrite for it even though the original was much loved by whoever read it. How's that for self-sabotage?

I refused to put in the work, refused to do anything hard. It was like my fight died that day on the bed. Only recently did I have a reason to fight again and that was for my twins. I had to fight for the roof over their head; I had to fight for the food in their belly; I had to fight for my time with them. Because of my twins, I realized my value and my worth. I walked away from a career in teaching that people said was "good" because it wasn't good to or for me.

When you don't put yourself first, you sabotage any chance you have of being your best self. You don't believe me? Try putting yourself first.

 REFLECTION TIME

Are you trapped in something that is not good for you because other people think it is? Do you let other people "should" on you? Have you walked away from your dreams, saying "Someday, I will [fill in the blank]", "One day, I will [fill in the blank]", "If only, I could [fill in the blank]"? Self-sabotage.

When you wake up in the morning, do you feel grateful for that gift of another day? Do you then think about all the stuff you have to do for other people or do you think about things that you want to do for you?

_____

_____

_____

_____

_____

_____

_____

_____

_____

_____

_____

_____

_____

_____

_____

_____

_____

_____

_____

Self-sabotage comes in many different forms. Maybe you are a substance abuser; maybe you're using drugs or alcohol to hide; maybe you self-harm. Maybe you overwork. Maybe you want to hide from pain or memories. Maybe you want to hide from the fact that you have not put yourself first and you are not where you want to be because you are scared to do so. You have only one life to live and you owe it to yourself to rock.

## (Case of the) Uns

Maybe the problem isn't just self-sabotage. Maybe you also have a case of the Uns. Do you feel undervalued? Do you feel undesirable? Do you feel unhappy? Are you unfeeling? Are you unhinged? Are you unstable? Have you become unpleasant? Do you think you're unnoticeable? Have you become unmerciful? Are you unrestrained? Are you unprogressive? Unproductive? Do you feel unappealing? Unpretty? Are you feeling unpurposed? Unqualified? Unappreciated? Unsafe? Is your mind unsettled? Unsteady? Unfocused?

Do you find what happened to you to be unspeakable? Are you unsure of who you are and where you're going and what you're doing and why you're here? Has it left you feeling untouchable? Uncomfortable? Unwanted?

Well I'm here to tell you that the case of the Uns is not unbeatable. You can change the dialog that is running through your mind. You can change who you think you are. You can change the way you feel. You have to change because yesterday is yesterday and today is all you have. And if you don't, your todays will be a repeat of yesterday.

Yes, you didn't leave that incident unscathed. There is something that happened to you. Maybe your heart got a little hardened or maybe you're afraid. Maybe your sex life is unpleasant or even nonexistent. But here's the wonderful thing: while yesterday cannot be unwritten, tomorrow is yet unwritten. Today you hold the pen to stroke the lines of your future. You are unshackled to your past if you choose to be. Life is about choices. And, unfortunately, you have a hard one to make. You will be challenged to change but change can be a beautiful part of that **challenge**.

You have to live your life unapologetically. Don't say sorry for anything that did not serve you purposefully. Don't be sorry for what happened to you. Don't be sorry for your role in it. Don't be sorry for existing. Don't be sorry for hurting. Don't be sorry for your anger. Don't be sorry for your fear. Don't be sorry for feeling trapped. Don't be sorry for anything that doesn't serve you. Live your life unapologetically. Go out and enjoy your life! **CHAlleNGE** yourself! Rock!

 REFLECTION TIME

Take a real assessment of your life. What Uns are you living with? Where did they come from? How can you change that? What does living unapologetically look like to you?

_____

_____

_____

_____

_____

_____

_____

_____

_____

_____

_____

_____

_____

_____

_____

_____

_____

## Can't

The word "can't" is such a strong word. When you use the word can't, you're saying that you are physically unable to do something. "I can't forget." Fine, don't forget. Who asked you to? I'm not asking you to. I'm not even telling you that it's possible to forget. Our brains are super computers. They absorb information and they hold on to it. There is no forgetting in the true sense of the word. There is only selective recall. So I'm not saying that you can forget what happened to you.

But I am saying you need to forgive yourself for what happened to you. I'm saying that you need to forgive the person because they will have to deal with that later on in life. Forgiveness does not mean staying silent; if you're brave enough to speak up, *please* do so. Nor does it mean putting yourself in harms way or forcing yourself to be in your perpetrator's presence. Protect yourself. However, your anger, your hatred, your fear only hurts you. As Malachy McCourt states, "Resentment is like taking poison and waiting for the other person to die". This is the exact quote that was shared with me many years ago when I made the connection with a church. Right then and there I drafted a letter of forgiveness to my rapist. What followed was me getting in touch with him and telling him about the hell he put me through for a few minutes of his pleasure. So don't tell me you can't forgive. Forgiveness is going to take work but, if you want to, you can do it. And you don't need to go as far as contacting the person who hurt you. You can write out a letter then burn it, releasing the emotions to the universe.

Look at the other places you allow that word, "can't", to

pervade. You can't go back to school because you're too old, too poor, too lost. You can't lose weight because you have to eat to live. You can't travel out of the country alone because you won't have protection. You can't trust other men because of what one person did to you. You can't trust yourself to make the right choices, to speak up for yourself because you failed to do so before.

Don't tell me you can't live your life. Living takes work and if you want to, you can. Don't tell me that you can't move on. Moving on takes work and, if you want to, you can. There is almost nothing in this life that we can't do if we desire and we are driven to make it happen. But it's not enough just want change. You need to rock.

Are you ready to rock?

 REFLECTION TIME

What excuses for living an unfulfilled life have you given yourself? What are your can'ts? What will you do about them to turn them into cans?

_____

_____

_____

_____

_____

_____

_____

_____

_____

_____

_____

_____

_____

_____

_____

_____

_____

_____

_____

_____

_____

## Keeping out

Keeping out is in direct opposition to rocking. Remember, when I told you to rock, I told you to connect to something outside of yourself. In the Cycle of Suck, you are keeping out what you need to connect to. Here you're keeping out your friends, your family, people who can help, things you enjoy, ways that you can connect. You are keeping out all of those positive relationships and experiences.

But you know what else you're doing? You're keeping *in* all those negative things that don't serve you. Those negative words you say to yourself, those negative emotions that are all wrapped up in what happened-- the hurt, the shame, the anger, the fear, become trapped inside of you. And you're also keeping in who you were born to be.

By keeping out love, friends, family, joy, connection, you're keeping yourself locked into the cycle of suck. You need to break the cycle. You've got to break away from the self-sabotage, break away from the case of the uns, break away from the word "can't", and break away from keeping out to keep in. You deserve much more from life than a permanent moment in time that you can't scrub out with an eraser. And you deserve much more from yourself.

The world is waiting for a person just like you, a person with your gifts and talents and voice. How can you get in the position to serve the world, to be a positive influence if you're keeping in what this world so desperately needs—the real you? Just as my students made me aware of the way I was limiting myself with my teaching career, think about the ways you are limiting yourself.

Do you want to suck or do you want to rock? The choice is and has always been yours.

 REFLECTION TIME

What have you been keeping out? What have you been keeping in? How are you limiting yourself? What can you do to fix this?

_____

_____

_____

_____

## GIVING YOURSELF PERMISSION

_____

_____

_____

_____

_____

_____

_____

_____

_____

_____

_____

_____

_____

_____

_____

_____

_____

_____

_____

_____

_____

# 4 GET YOUR LIFE BACK

Now this final chapter of the book is about what you can do with your life right now in order to get out of the cycle of suck and into a rocking life.

**Get help.**

One of the most important things to do from this point forward is to seek help from a counselor, a therapist, a psychologist, or a psychiatrist-- whichever one you need. It's not about medicine and it's not about having a mental illness or weakness. It is about finding a way to create a support system and a coping mechanism that actually works.

Before I realized that I needed to talk to someone, I did not cope with the rape very well at all. I told you about the promiscuity. I told you about the failure at school. But what I didn't tell you about is my crying out. One of the reasons I failed my first year of college is because that was the same year I discovered the internet and chat rooms. I'm not talking about an Al Gore type of discovery. I was coming from a place where we didn't have computers in the home to a school that had several computer labs.

There I was on the internet. I created my first email through Excite mail and there were these chat rooms where all these anonymous people gathered together online. They didn't know me; they didn't know my story; they didn't have a way to prejudge me. It was such a safe place for me to spill one of the heaviest subjects I could foist onto some unsuspecting cyber soul. All I knew was how heavy it weighed on my heart and my mind that I didn't think about how heavy it was to drop in someone's lap. And they responded the way I wished that girl did those years ago when I first told someone what happened.

Those unknown souls in the chat room would immediately give me their condolences and would ask me if I was ok. They would ask me to tell them the story. And whenever they asked if he was in jail, I would move on to the next chat room.

I repeated this cycle for an entire semester, missing class after class. It was addicting. I was crying out. I needed to be heard. I needed my feelings validated. I needed someone to say what happened was wrong. But, what I was not prepared to face was why I did not seek persecution.

Once that girl laughed at me, I felt the rest of the world would too. I felt that people would hate me, especially the ones I swore I loved. I already had trouble with my mother. My father already abandoned me. I already felt different and like an outcast. So whenever I could not answer the question, "Is he in jail" with the right answer, which should have been "Yes", I would then run because I never fully understood why I allowed that one girl to shut me up.

The best place for me to talk was not inside of cyberspace. I should have been in someone's office getting the help I needed from someone who was trained to help me. So I'm telling you now get help. That was the best advice I could have ever received. And that is the best advice that I can give you now. Get help. Don't go at this alone. Don't drop this in the laps of people who are not equipped to handle it and to help you. Get help.

If you don't know where to find help, there are plenty of resources online. If you go to the Rape Abuse & Incest National Network (RAINN), which you can find at rainn.org, one of their first tabs says, "Get help". And, if you click on it, the page will tell you to get help *now*. There are so many resources there for you-- the National Sexual Assault Hotline, the National Sexual Assault Online Hotline, a hot link to find a local counseling center. There's help there so if you want it, you can have it. Get help.

If you're in college, go to your counseling center. The visit should be covered by your tuition and fees. *Get help*. Even if you don't have insurance, call around until you can find a center that does see patients on a sliding scale because the most important thing you can do for yourself is to get help.

If you're someone who feels that your calling now is to provide help, just two tabs away on the RAINN website is another tab that says, "Get involved". You can join the hotline as a trained responder. You can volunteer for RAINN. You can find a way to form or participate in a support group on campus. You can donate to centers.

I know I'm only talking about RAINN right now but there are lots of places to get help and to help. When I was doing research for this book, I clicked through so many Facebook pages, liking them so that I could get updated information and stay up on the laws that are passed. It's really important, if you're past the stage of hurting and you're in the stage of wanting to help, that you stay informed and that you reach out. There are people waiting for you, for your story, for your very embodiment of survival to help them move forward in their life.

**Create a vision board.**

Something else you can do for yourself is dream again. I don't mean just in your mental space. I am talking about grabbing a poster board and some magazines, then going on an arts and crafts journey of creating your vision board. Now I don't want you thinking too far into the future; I want you thinking about just the very next year. Your thought should be, "Over the next 12 months, what positivity do I want to attract into my life".

Now vision boards are my favorite things to create. When I was a teacher, I made sure my students did one every single year and I like to think they loved making them as much as I did.

On your vision board, I want you to mainly use images. They can be images with symbolic meaning or they can even be words that empower you. But I don't want you to write on your vision board. I want you to connect to something outside of yourself. So search & find these things in magazines, make connections, and then put them on your board. It doesn't have to be a big board; it can be the size of paper or it can be the size of a small poster. It can even be a cereal box opened up. Yeah I had some creative students.

But I want you to get a vision. I want you to see a life filled with positivity and action.

**Write down your goals.**

I want you to write out your goals. Make them visible. Outline them in chunks then put bulleted action steps right beneath each goal. For example, if you want to go back to school, don't just say, "Go back to school". If you have a particular school in mind, then you write down that school. If you have a couple of schools in mind, then you write them both. Your next action step is to decide on a major. The next action step is to make sure you understand the requirements and that you do what it takes to meet them. If an SAT is required, then you prepare, study, and take an SAT. Next step, complete an application. Then you meet with a school advisor. Whatever those action steps are that fit your goal, that is what you do. You need to outline them so that you can check them off as you do them.

Goals example:
1.  Go to My State University
    a.  Business Administration major
    b.  SAT score of 1200/ACT score of 24
    c.  Complete application
    d.  Get two letters of recommendation
    e.  Write college essay
    f.  Turn in application
    g.  Meet with school advisor
    h.  Fill out financial aid form
2.  Become a ToastMaster
    a.  Find a local chapter
    b.  ….

## Develop Positive Mantras.

The next thing you're going to do is develop positive mantras-- "I am" statements. So whatever those negative feelings are that you have, flip them. Instead of saying, "I am unworthy," you will now say, "I am worthy". Instead of saying, "I am ugly," you will now say, "I am beautiful". Instead of saying, "I was stupid," you will now say, "I am brilliant". Instead of saying, "I don't deserve anything good," you will now say, "I am deserving of everything good".

So develop your mantras. You can have three "I am" statements; you can have five "I am" statements. You will put these where you can see them-- on your phone, on your mirror, on your folder, on the back of the bathroom door, etc. You will put them everywhere. And every time you pass by them, every time you see them, you will stop and say them. If you're by a mirror, you will stop and say them while looking into your eyes.

You will stop the negative talk. Anytime something negative comes up, rebut it with something positive. Anytime you start to feel hurt or scared, think of a time when you didn't. If you don't have a time like that, then it's time to imagine a life that will combat those feelings, a life of beautiful positive light overpowering the darkness. The life you outlined in your goals and created on your vision board.

## Reach out.

One of the final things that I'm going to outline in this book is about reaching out to those closest to you-- a cousin, a friend, a family member, etc. Make those connections. Reach out and talk to them.

## Write your story.

Remember I said you need to own your story? When you reach the end of this book, I want you to pick up the pen and grab a pad of paper. Then I want you to pour out your story, unapologetically. Don't edit. Don't stop. Write it all the way out. As you do, feel its hold loosening up on you. The more you tell your story, the less power it will hold over you.

## Practice an attitude of gratitude.

Now I'm not talking about being grateful for having a traumatic event happen to you. No, I'm talking about being grateful for the week that was before you. Find anything, no matter how small or even how large it may be, and write it down in your gratitude journal.

I want you to keep a year-long gratitude journal. In it, you will list your three "I am" statements. "I am beautiful"; "I am smart"; "I am worthy"; "I am [fill in the blank]". Then you will write down the one thing that you are grateful for from that week. You'll explain why you're grateful for it and what it means to your life. Don't skip this part and don't skip a week.

By the end of the year, you will have 52 reasons to be grateful for your life and gratitude is essential to being connected to your life.

One thing I am grateful for is that I'm around to watch my children chase butterflies. It is singularly the most enjoyable moment of my day. I get to watch them run around with freedom, careless abandonment, and enjoyment. In those brief moments, I remember what it's like to be a kid with the world wide open.

So look back over your week and think of one thing for which you can be grateful. Doesn't have to be something you did-- it can be, but it can also be something outside of yourself. And to help you get started, I'm giving you FREE journal pages for the first 13 weeks of your gratitude year. Just enter bit.ly/GYPjournal into your favorite browser and download your free gift.

## REFLECTION TIME

Which of the suggestions in this chapter will you implement in your life? You don't have to do them all but doing at least three of them will help you have a fuller more enjoyable life.

_____

_____

_____

_____

_____

_____

_____

_____

_____

_____

_____

_____

_____

_____

_____

_____

_____

_____

That's it. I hope that, after reading this book, you give yourself permission to exit the Cycle of Suck and you give yourself permission to *rock*. I have great hopes for you. I know you're going to do wonderful things with the rest of your life. If no one else is there to tell you, then I'm going to tell you-- you are worthy of a wonderful life; you are worthy of a full and abundant life; you are worthy of a life created by your choices and on your own terms. So, if you're ready, give yourself permission to go R.O.C.K.! I'm already so proud of you! Oh, and don't forget to grab your FREE gratitude journal at bit.ly/GYPjournal.

## REFLECTION TIME

Write out your story.

_____

_____

_____

_____

_____

_____

_____

_____

_____

_____

_____

_____

_____

_____

_____

_____

_____

_____

_____

_____

## GIVING YOURSELF PERMISSION

_____
_____
_____
_____
_____
_____
_____
_____
_____
_____
_____
_____
_____
_____
_____
_____
_____
_____
_____
_____
_____
_____
_____

# ABOUT THE AUTHOR

Shaneequa Cannon, a graduate of the University of Miami, currently lives in Atlanta, though she travels often back to Miami where, after a decade of helping students believe in the possibilities of themselves, she finally followed her own advice and escaped from the confines of the classroom. She strongly believes that passion is what feeds you and purpose is what you do to feed others. So her mission is to use her time here on Earth wisely, helping to change and shape the lives of those who cross her path. She has become a Kinetic MindShift Coach, helping others step into their power with passion and purpose.

To book her for speaking engagements, you can contact Shaneequa at www.shaneequacannon.tv, reach out to her on various social media platforms as @ShaneequaCTV, or send her an email at ShaneequaSpeaks@gmail.com.